THE ZEN OF SLIME

When it comes to innovating with slime, the possibilities are endless.

—@sparklygoo

THE ZEN OF SLIME

A DIY INSPIRATION NOTEBOOK

@SPARKLYGOO (Prim Pattanaporn)

Alena Woods

FaLAB (Fallon and Aspen Ayala-Gregson)

The Countryman Press
A division of W. W. Norton & Company
Independent Publishers Since 1923

For information about permission to reproduce selections
from this book, write to Permissions, The Countryman
Press, 500 Fifth Avenue, New York, NY 10110

For information about special discounts for bulk purchases,
please contact W. W. Norton Special Sales at
specialsales@wwnorton.com or 800-233-4830

Manufacturing by Versa Press
Book design by Lidija Tomas
Production manager: Devon Zahn

The Countryman Press
www.countrymanpress.com

A division of W. W. Norton & Company, Inc.
500 Fifth Avenue, New York, NY 10110
www.wwnorton.com

978-1-68268-219-7 (pbk.)

10   9   8   7   6   5   4   3   2   1

An Important Note:

The "recipes" included in this book are for the production of nonedible slime only.

Borax, which can be significantly irritating to the skin of sensitive individuals, is not a required ingredient in slime, and every recipe in this book can be made borax-free. Where borax is called for in a recipe, you can replace it with laundry starch, laundry detergent, or contact lens solution mixed with a little baking soda.

If you choose to use borax, a diluted solution of not more than 1/2 teaspoon per cup of hot water may prove less irritating. Sensitivity to borax or other ingredients of slime may occur at any time, so readers are reminded to use common sense and refrain from incorporating in their slime any material to which they are likely to react. If you do become aware of skin irritation or any other adverse reaction at any point in the preparation of a recipe or in the course of using your slime, please stop and, if appropriate, seek medical advice.

CONTENTS

INTRODUCTION

Prim Pattanaporn • @sparklygoo

Art has always piqued my interest: As a small child, I was captivated by the unique art of cake decorating, particularly the use of fondant and modeling chocolate. I love the idea that edible things can be sculpted into something beautiful and sometimes become too pretty to eat—or in the case of slime, too perfect to play with (or eat). But I can never resist sticking my hands into the sticky goodness.

I remember watching my first slime video on Instagram and wanting to know what the concoction felt like. Was it squishy? Gooey? I had to know. I began looking for slime to purchase online, but sadly, no one was selling it at the time. I decided to take a leap of faith and try to make it on my own, but it was nowhere near as easy as I thought it would be. On my first attempt, the slime was rock hard; it was not at all comparable to the slime I saw in those videos. But I started to experiment with a variety of measurements until I achieved what I believed was the perfect texture. I now make up my own recipes, with unique ingredients and fun add-ins. I once experimented with air-dry clay and found out a way to give it a slime-like consistency by adding a few wet ingredients such as water and glue. I also love to put different trinkets, like cute erasers and faux candy made of resin, into my slime. When it comes to innovating with slime, the possibilities are endless.

Not only is slime fun to play with but is also therapeutic. The repetitive movement of kneading slime, which eventually becomes subconscious, keeps my hands busy and redirects my stress to the slime. When I am playing with slime, it's as if I enter a trance-like state of relaxation. I want to share this experience with you and help you create some of my favorite recipes, which I hope will help you destress and have fun. Once you have mastered the various recipes that this book offers, you'll not only have a collection of different textured slime to play with, but you'll be on your way to becoming a slime connoisseur! So . . . what are you waiting for?

THE BASICS

THE ALCHEMY OF SLIME
GETTING STARTED
BASIC RECIPES
TROUBLESHOOTING

THE ALCHEMY OF SLIME

The key to life is balance. Slime is no different. At the intersection of gooey, sticky, stretchy, and slushy lies the divine state of slime: an elusive form of matter so satisfying and wondrous its very existence defies explanation (again, like life). Actually, the science of slime is easily understood and the tools of its creation easy to obtain. What is more important, however, is the nature of slime.

Slime is more than a formula; it's a form of self-expression and self-knowledge. Given the same recipe and ingredients two bakers will produce two different pies, each reflecting the spirit and skill of its creator. So, too, will your slime be inseparable from your own nature. Begin your slime journey with an open and flexible attitude because, while the fun begins right away, it will take time for you to discover your inner slime nature and realize its true expression. The basic alchemy of slime will take minutes to learn, but its secrets and nuances will engage you for a lifetime—or at least few weeks.

Slime can be reduced to three essential elements: glue, water, and a thickening agent. Consider glue to be your base. By manipulating it we will release the slime qualities it already possesses. Just as a sculptor merely removes the excess marble from the statue that is already present in the stone, know that your slime is only waiting to be realized.

No pressure, but you shouldn't just leave it unrealized like that.

The polyvinyl acetate molecules within glue are the threads of your slime tapestry, loosely woven and just lying there, useless. Alone, the glue is runny, liquidy, and undignified. We've all been there. But, just as we all have a better self inside waiting to surface, so too does the glue have hidden potential. We add water, the basic element of life, to nurture the slime dormant in the glue, to tell it that we feel its presence, that we get what it's really trying to be, that we're not judging how it looks right now.

Once the connection between the slime and the self is established, we add a thickener, like borax or another liquid starch, to impart form and substance to the slime. The agent bonds the latent threads of the glue, weaving those lazy molecules into a beautiful tapestry.

Now a strong and malleable material, the slime is ready to be molded like a young mind. Manipulate the slime with your hands, making it your own. It will respond to your will: If you are tough on it the slime will become durable and resilient; treat it gently and it will become pliable and trusting. It's like raising a child, but with way less pressure.

Now that you have created slime, you have realized yourself. Hope that was okay; it wasn't supposed to awaken anything dark in you. But this is only the beginning. You will reach a point of change in your life, or you will re-create yourself, and therefore your slime must change. You don't want some old slime that just doesn't go with your vibe anymore. Dissolve your slime in vinegar to unravel its molecular threads. Now you can begin this work again and weave an updated, more appropriate slime tapestry that reflects the new, wiser you.

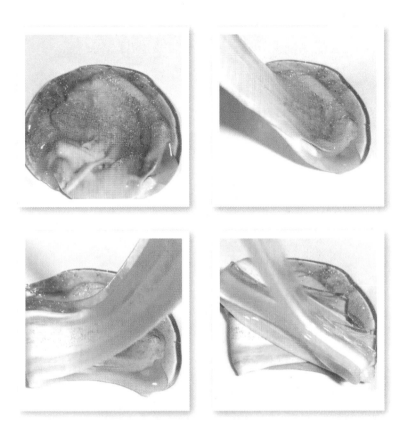

*A little magic can take
you a long way.*

—Roald Dahl

GETTING STARTED

MUST-HAVES FOR SMOOTH AND FLUFFY SLIMES

- Glue (white or clear)
- Liquid starch
- Laundry detergent
- Borax dissolved in water (see safety note on page 5)
- Contact solution
- Baking soda
- Wooden spoon or spatula
- Shaving cream—the "foamy" style works the best
- At least one mixing bowl (large enough to fit both hands)
- Food coloring
- Foamy liquid soap
- Measuring spoons and cups
- Plastic bags or containers in which to store the finished slime (see pages 91–101 on ways to package and sell your slime)

EXTRAS

- Styrofoam microbeads, for making "floam," and adding texture
- Plastic pellets, for crunchy fishbowl slime
- Glitter or sequins, if sparkles are your thing
- Metallic paint, if you want your slime to shine
- Tiny figurines/toys, such as flowers, to lay on top for design
- Tiny beads
- Scented lotions
- Shampoo
- Glitter glue
- Star confetti
- Tiny pompoms
- Fluorescent paint
- Tiny Japanese erasers
- Crayola Model Magic modeling clay—the magic ingredient for butter slime

BASIC RECIPES

BASIC BORAX-FREE SLIME

If you're a first-time slimer, starting out with this basic slime recipe will have you feeling like a pro in no time. You can replace the contact solution with laundry detergent. The scent is divine!

What you'll need:
½ cup white school glue
½ tablespoon baking soda
Food coloring (optional)
Contact solution

1. Pour your glue and baking soda into a large mixing bowl and mix with a silicon spatula until well combined. This is the time to add food coloring if you'd like!
2. Start adding your contact solution, little by little, while stirring your mixture with a spatula. If you add too much solution at once, your slime will become too hard.
3. Smooth out any lumps in your slime and add more contact solution if the mixture is too sticky.
4. Knead the slime with your hands and enjoy! Store your creation in an airtight container or bag when you're ready to save it for later.

BORAX-FREE CLEAR SLIME (LIQUID GLASS)

This slime is a great base for many of the fun slime recipes that come later in this book. Additions like sequins and beads are easily seen in this glass-like slime. You can also add a touch of color to mimic water.

What you'll need:
½ cup clear school glue
½ tablespoon baking soda
Contact solution

1. Pour your glue and baking soda into a large mixing bowl and mix with a silicon spatula until well combined.
2. Start adding your contact solution, little by little, while stirring your mixture with a spatula. If you add too much solution at once, your slime will become too hard.
3. Smooth out any lumps in your slime and add more contact solution if the mixture is too sticky.
4. You'll need to store your clear slime in an airtight container for a few days, so that it can set and become less cloudy.

CLEAR SLIME (WITH BORAX)

With this recipe, you won't have to wait for your slime to set, but the chemical activator, borax, can cause a mild skin irritation if handled for a long period of time. Do not ingest or use in large quantities.

What you'll need:
½ cup clear school glue
2 cups hot water
½ teaspoon borax

1. Pour your glue into a medium mixing bowl.
2. Add the hot water to a second bowl and stir the borax. Wait for the borax to dissolve, then begin adding the mixture to the glue, one teaspoon at a time. Keep mixing until the mixture is not very sticky and you like its consistency.
3. When you're happy with your slime, enjoy playing with it. Store in an airtight container or bag.

FLUFFY SLIME

You're going to love the consistency of this slime, and how easy it is to make.

What you'll need:
4 cups shaving cream
Food coloring (optional)
½ cup white school glue
½ teaspoon baking soda
1 tablespoon contact solution

1. Measure out 4 cups of shaving cream and pour into a large mixing bowl.
2. If you'd like, add some food coloring and mix it into the shaving cream until combined.
3. Once the cream is your desired color, add your glue along with a small pinch of baking soda and mix until thoroughly combined.
4. Add your contact solution and stir it all together. Whip together the solution until it's fluffy; you might have to add more contact solution to the mix if it's still too sticky.
5. Take your slime out of the bowl and start kneading it with your hands!
6. Once you're done reveling in its cloud-like consistency, store it in an airtight container.

You can't use up creativity. The more you use, the more you have.

—Maya Angelou

TROUBLESHOOTING

Slime doesn't gel:

Try adding more of the liquid starch or borax solution, if you're using this. You may need to add more borax to the water and make sure the borax solution is not too hot.

Too liquidy:

Add more liquid bleach solution or borax solution, if using, and make sure it is not hot. If it is in the sun or has been outside, it has to be cooled to room temperature before handling.

Sooo . . . sticky:

If your slime is sticky, add more contact solution and knead it until you are happy with texture. If you add too much, it will get hard.

Color is streaking—not intentionally:

If color is not consistent throughout, try adding the food coloring earlier on in the process, even before mixing in your thickening agent. Color blends better when it is liquid, but a lot of kneading of the slime will also ensure consistency of color.

Hard like rubber:

Unfortunately, that one is usually a deal-breaker. I'd toss it, but you could try adding more glue and water first.

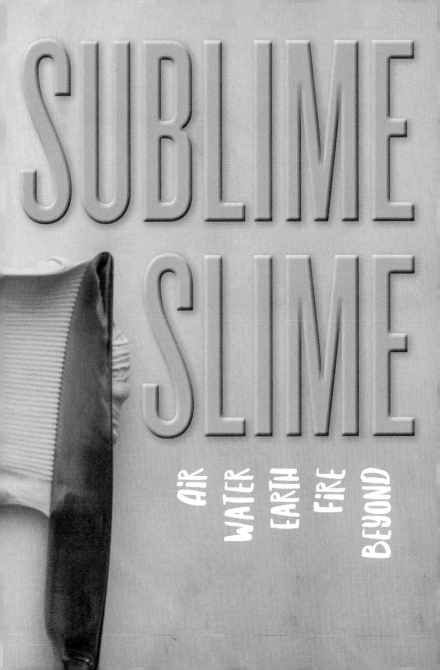

AiR

PEGASUS

•

GALAXY GOO

•

UNICORN BOOGERS

•

STARRY NIGHT

•

UNICORN SHIMMER

•

RAINBOW SLIME

PEGASUS

RECIPE

What you'll need:
Clear slime (pages 19–20)
Extra fine pink glitter

1. Follow the recipe for one of our clear slimes in the Basic Recipes section. If you opt for the borax-free slime, remember to let your slime sit for a few days in an airtight container.
2. Fold in your extra fine glitter when your slime has set. When you are finished, put it back in the container!

your wings already exist.
All you have to do is fly.

GALAXY GOO

TIP

If you want your
slime to look iridescent,
you have a few choices. You can use
metallic or pearl paint, or, raid your makeup
collection and use that glitter eyeshadow that
you wore once to a party. Just pop out the disk
of color, crush it up, and add to your slime.

great slime is a work in progress.

UNICORN BOOGERS

NAME
@sparklygoo

STARTING OUT
After multiple big accounts that each
have a few million followers started
reposting my videos, I started gaining a
massive following.

FILMING SLIME
I film and edit all my videos on my
phone. I like filming with nice and clean
settings, so I use my white desk
as the background.

*Born to ride
unicorns*

STARRY NIGHT

slime mixing is a beautiful thing

NAME
Sensory for the Soul

MOTTO
A slime shop dripping with aesthetic

WHY SLIME?
Sensory experiences can be very calming
and can help you work through troubling
emotions, such as anxiety or frustration.
Working with materials that require
pressure and manipulation can release
physical energy or tension.

UNICORN SHIMMER

NAME
Monstrous Things

STARTING OUT
When I decided to start an Etsy shop selling party favors, I knew slime would be the first thing I started stocking. It has taken off and been such a huge seller that I devote my entire shop to slime.

MOST POPULAR SLIME
Unicorn Shimmer, with large, iridescent glitter

FAVORITE ADD-INS
Foam beads
Glitter flakes

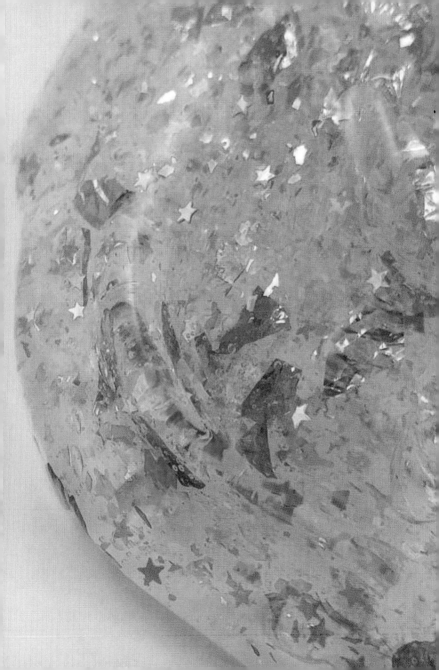

RAINBOW SLIME

To get a rainbow effect, divide your slime into 3 or 4 small bowls. Tint each with food coloring or metallic paint in the colors of the rainbow. Gently pull out each color separately into a long ribbon, then allow the strands to come together. Rainbow slime is fun to make, but, just like a rainbow, it won't last. The colors will eventually run together.

TIP

Lighting and creativity are very important! Create a signature slime if you can. Set the trend! Go crazy with it.

—*@sparklygoo*

When it rains,
look for rainbows.

WATER

SUSHI

·

MERMAID

·

SEA GLASS

·

JELLYFISH HEART

·

FISH PEBBLES

·

OCEAN SWIRL GLITTER

·

SEA FLOAM

·

FISH IN A BAG

SUSHI

NAME
FaLAB

STARTING OUT
Our favorite part of the slime-making process is decorating a slime, because you can transform such a plain white slime into something amazing and pleasing to the eye.

FAVORITE ADD-INS
We love adding glitter to clear slimes. For opaque slimes, our favorite add-in is colorful "floam" beads! It just looks so cute!

BUSINESS SENSE
If you're selling slime, create quality products, take good pictures and videos, post regularly, and have good customer service.

TIP
Make sure to provide some kind of activator to ensure that your customers can fix their slime if it gets sticky during shipping.

Having an online shop has become our generation's "lemonade stand."

—FaLAB

MERMAID

ADD-INS TO MAKE
MERMAID SLIME SHINE

Glitter

Metallic paint

Food coloring

TIPS

You can add your glitter just before your potion turns to slime, or you can knead in glitter, which is really pretty—lots of instagrammers do this and show the process. If you want to do it that way, leave your slime in a container for a day or two first so it gets a little firmer.

SEAGLASS

sea glass represents the magic of transformation

JELLYFISH HEART

NAME
@Slime.Jewel

MOST POPULAR SLIME
Clear! Everyone loves clear; it's just so visually pleasing. I think people like clear slime because of how pretty it looks when it traps the light, kind of like the ocean.

FAVORITE ADD-IN
Holographic glitter is forever my favorite

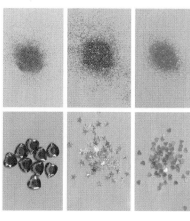

TIP

Give your slime extra time. Sometimes I think I failed at a batch and I let it sit overnight . . . it always turns out perfectly.

FISH PEBBLES

RECIPE

What you'll need:
1 (5-ounce) bottle clear glue
2 cups hot water
½ teaspoon borax
Handful of fish pebbles

1. Pour your glue into a medium mixing bowl.
2. Add your hot water to a second bowl and stir the borax. Wait for the borax to dissolve, then begin adding the mixture to the glue, one teaspoon at a time. Keep mixing until the mixture is not very sticky and you like its consistency.
3. Now add fish pebbles until they've coated the top of your slime. Your concoction shouldn't be too tough to mix at this point; you'll finish mixing and activating your slime while you stir in the pebbles.
4. When you're happy with your slime, enjoy playing with it or store it in an airtight container or bag.

OCEAN SWIRL
GLITTER

My favorite moment is when I have a new recipe idea

NAME

Slimeza

STARTING OUT

I've fallen into a kind of obsession with slime. I discovered it while I was looking for a Christmas present for my little brother, and I started ordering a lot of slime online for myself. I was spending so much money on it that I decided to make my own.

MOST POPULAR SLIME

Galaxy slime, with deep blue, a bit of purple, a lot of glitter, and pearl powder has been a big success. It's super pretty. Pearl powder really adds magic to your slime. It gives a sense of depth.

MAKING SLIME

I make a large quantity of clear slime at one time to use as a base for the different slimes I sell. There is always a moment where I have a few pounds of slime in my hand and I have to play with it to mix it well. It feels like a sport and it's a great arm workout! For each recipe, I add ingredients to my base and see a new slime come to life.

TIPS

You've probably heard about using borax to make slime. I have some that I sometimes use to fix my slime texture, but I don't use it often. Start by using laundry detergent, which is way easier to work with. No mess, it has a nice smell, and it will really help you make a non-sticky slime. When you mix your glue and your laundry detergent, don't be afraid to see it get messy. Just keep your slime in a container until it is perfectly mixed. Add laundry detergent until you get confident with the texture, without stickiness. You will perfect the texture later, when you knead it.

SEA FLOAM

RECIPE

What you'll need:
1 (5-ounce) bottle clear glue
1 teaspoon borax, dissolved in 1 cup warm water
2 drops blue food coloring
Glitter
Foam beads

1. Pour glue into large bowl. Add activator (borax water) a few teaspoons at a time until the glue begins to come together like slime.

2. Add food coloring to desired hue. Mix and knead, adding additional drops of activator as needed.

3. Once the clear slime is mixed, you can let it sit in container for 3 days or until bubbles disappear. (You don't have to do this but it makes a prettier slime.)

4. When you're ready, knead in glitter carefully, to not make more bubbles.

5. Dunk slime into foam beads and knead in until it is crunchy. Shape into squares for fun.

RECIPE

What you'll need:

Small plastic bags
Clear slime (pages 19–20)
Green food coloring
Glitter
Small plastic fish toys
Twine

1. Set up each bag by placing it into a drinking glass and folding the top over the rim, so it's easy to put the slime into the bag.
2. Prepare your slime by mixing it with just a drop of color. Also add glitter in ocean colors.
3. Put one bit of slime in the bottom of the bag, to go about ¼ of the way up.
4. Add fish.
5. Top with slime to cover.
6. Tie off bag with twine.

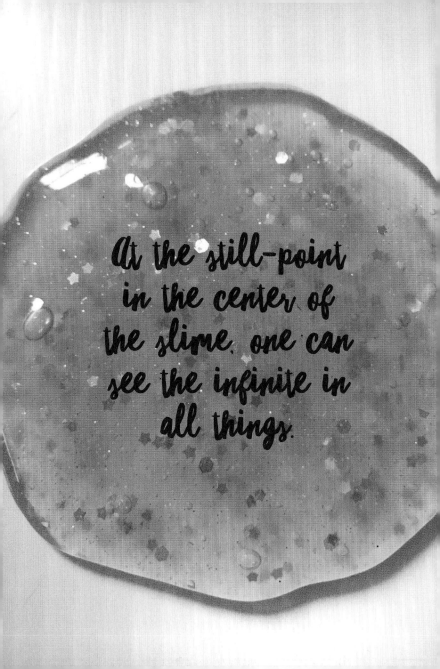

At the still-point
in the center of
the slime, one can
see the infinite in
all things.

EARTH

FRUIT CONFETTI

•

GREEN GOLD

•

ARCTIC

•

FRUITY FLOAMS AND SLIME

•

JASMINE GREEN TEA

•

DINOSAUR SLIME

FRUIT CONFETTI

NAME
M and J Slime Factory

MOST POPULAR SLIME
Our most popular is our aqua
that we made by mistake when
trying to make green. The aqua
color was really pretty and we
put it in our store with some fruit
confetti—the rest is history.

FAVORITE ADD-IN
Fruit confetti

Relax about your mistakes; Good things come from being imperfect.

Make sure to package your slime so it won't spill and use something airtight so it won't harden.

GREEN GOLD

Gold leaf is beautiful suspended in a clear slime. Just knead the gold leaf flakes into the slime as it's coming together.

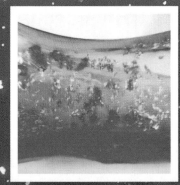

Green is the prime color of the world, and that from which its loveliness arises.

—Pedro Calderon de la Barca

ARCTIC

NAME
Carly Rose

STARTING OUT
I saw all of the slime videos online and I was so intrigued. I was so curious about how they felt! Now I love making slime. It's always a fun process.

FAVORITE ADD-IN
I love trying out new scents like different essential oils.

Be unique.
People will follow.

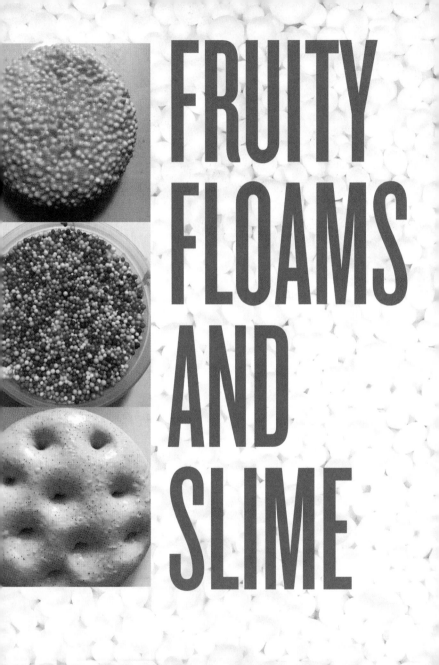

FRUITY FLOAMS AND SLIME

NAME
Peachy Slime Bakery

FAVORITE ADD-INS
Styrofoam balls for texture

JASMINE
GREEN TEA

Bread and water
could so easily be
toast and tea

NAME
CBSlimes

FAVORITE ADD-INS
Jasmine essential oil
Plastic pellet beads—they
add a nice crunching sound
to your slime and it feels
really good when you're
playing with it.

TIP

If you fail at making
slime the first
time (this usually
happens), just keep
trying and you will
get better.

DINOSAUR SLIME

RECIPE

What you'll need:

4 tablespoons clear
   school glue
⅛ teaspoon baking soda
Contact lens solution
1 drop green food
   coloring
2 plastic dinosaurs

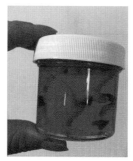

1. Add the clear school glue to a bowl. Add the baking soda and 1 drop of green food coloring, and mix well.
2. Slowly add contact lens solution until the slime is no longer sticky and is manageable.
3. Add two plastic dinosaurs and you have dinosaur slime!
4. Store the slime in an airtight container when you're done admiring your creation.

What made me want to start making slime was a YouTube video—the slime looked super fun, pretty, and squishy.

—@CBSlimes

TIP

Try not to add too much
baking soda and contact
lens solution—it will ruin the
texture of your slime.

Lava never
falls in the
wrong place

FiRE

VOLCANIC ROCK

•

DRAGON SCALE
GLITTER

•

CINDER(ELLA)

•

MOLTEN GOLD

•

LAVA

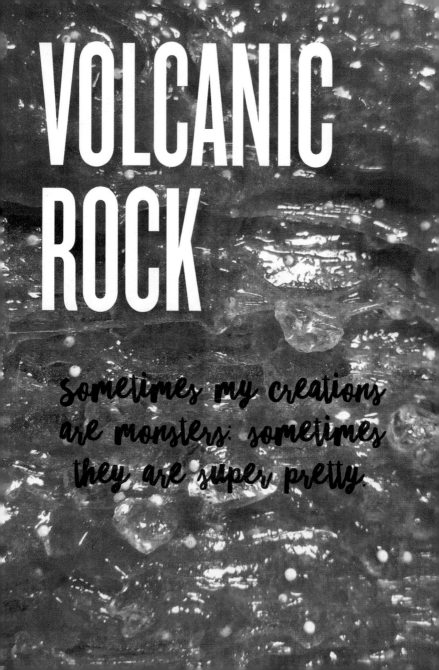

VOLCANIC ROCK

sometimes my creations are monsters; sometimes they are super pretty.

RECIPE

What you'll need:

Clear slime (pages 19–20)
Red aquarium glass crystals
Styrofoam filler beads

1. Follow the recipe for one of our clear slimes in the Basic Recipes section.
2. To make extra crunchy Volcanic Rock Slime, add red aquarium glass crystals and a small amount of Styrofoam filler beads to the clear slime. The glass will give the slime its color and the foam beads make the slime very pretty. I try to use as little slime as I can, to make it as crunchy as possible.

TIP

If you want to create new effects and new recipes, try not to add too many different colors or texturing ingredients. It's like in fashion or graphic design—too many colors and elements mixed together get ugly. Make it simple. And from that simple slime that you like, try different add-ins and you'll find something that will make you happy.

—*Slimeza*

DRAGON SCALE GLITTER

It simply isn't an adventure worth telling if there aren't any dragons.

—J.R.R. Tolkien

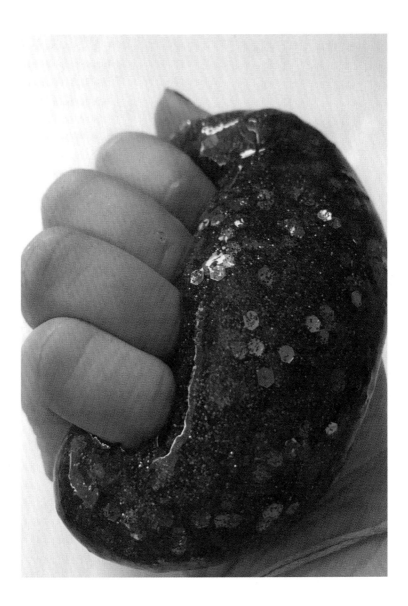

CINDER(ELLA)

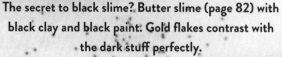

The secret to black slime? Butter slime (page 82) with black clay and black paint. Gold flakes contrast with the dark stuff perfectly.

MOLTEN GOLD

Meditation is the golden key to all the mysteries of life.

LAVA

Enthusiasm is a volcano on whose top never grows the grass of hesitation.

—Khalil Gibran

flow with whatever
may happen, and let your
mind be free.

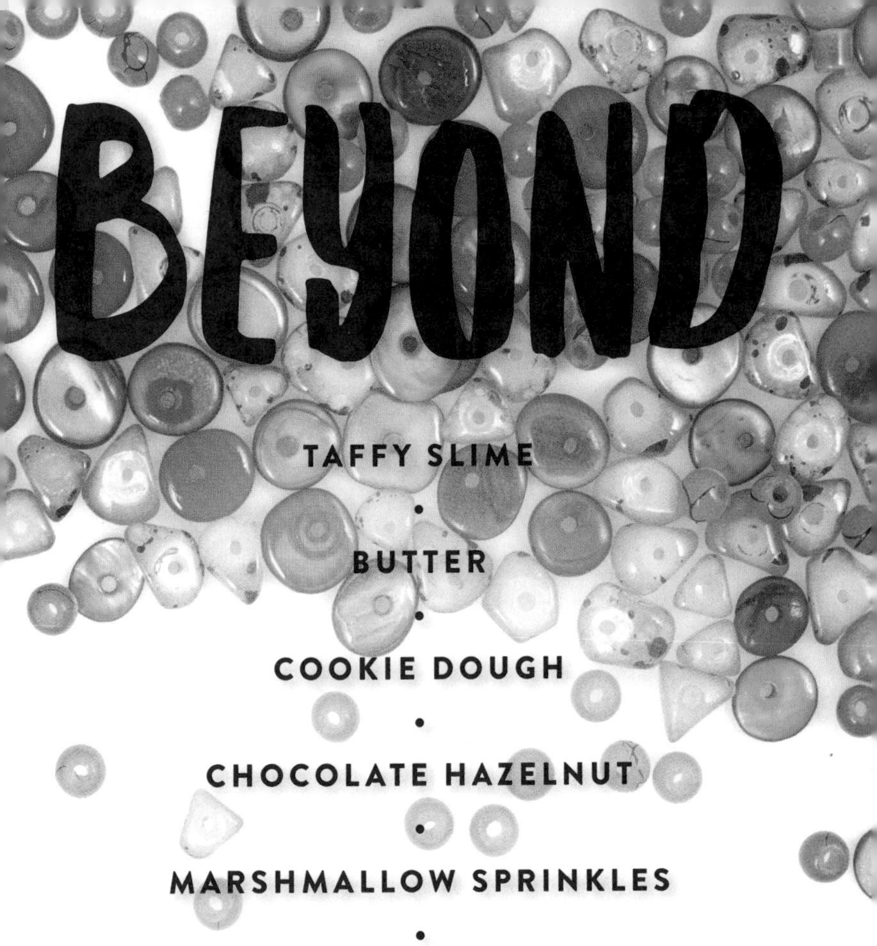

BEYOND

TAFFY SLIME

•

BUTTER

•

COOKIE DOUGH

•

CHOCOLATE HAZELNUT

•

MARSHMALLOW SPRINKLES

•

VANILLA WHIPPED CREAM

•

STRAWBERRY CRUNCH

•

BANANA CRUNCH

TAFFY SLIME

BUTTER

RECIPE

What you'll need:

½ cup white glue
About ½ cup soft
    modeling clay
½ teaspoon borax,
    dissolved in 2 cups
    hot water
Pastel food coloring

1. Mix glue with borax solution, about a teaspoon at a time, until it clumps into slime.
2. Knead a 1:1 ratio of modeling or soft clay to slime, until it is fully combined.
3. Use a butter knife to spread your "butter" and have fun.

COOKIE
DOUGH

This is a nonedible Nutella®-style slime. We think it looks like the real thing!

CHOCOLATE HAZELNUT

RECIPE

What you'll need:
½ cup white glue
Brown paint
½ cup laundry detergent

1. Pour the glue into a large bowl. Add the brown paint, a little bit at a time, until it is the color of Nutella.
2. Add laundry detergent and mix until it comes together as slime. If it's too sticky, add more laundry detergent.
3. **Do not eat this!**

MARSHMALLOW
SPRINKLES

VANILLA WHIPPED CREAM

RECEIPE

what you'll need:
1 package Crayola magic
    model clay
½ cup glue
⅓ cup foaming soap
Vanilla extract, for scent
Rubber gloves, for mixing

1. Put one 1 package of
   Crayola magic model clay
   into a large mixing bowl.
2. Add ½ cup glue.
3. Use rubber gloves to
   knead/mix the mixture
   until you achieve sticky
   paste-like consistency.
   Make sure to knead out
   any lumps.
4. Add ⅓ cup foaming soap,
   ¼ cup water, and dash of
   vanilla extract, if using,
   to the mixture. Continue
   to knead until the slime
   absorbs all the liquid.

This recipe is one of my most treasured secrets— and I'm sharing it here with you!

—@sparklygoo

STRAWBERRY
CRUNCH

My first hit was sparkly strawberry Crunch!

—@sparklygoo

Add deliciously fruity scents to these crunchy slimes, with shampoos or foamy hand soap. These are clear slimes with glitter, food coloring, and foam balls. Shape them into squares and balls for fun.

BANANA CRUNCH

PRESENTATION
IS EVERYTHING

ENTREPRENEUR 101

PHOTOGRAPHING
SLIME

CLEANUP

WHERE TO BUY
SUPPLIES

PRESENTATION IS EVERYTHING

We are Fallon and Aspen of FaLAB in Las Vegas and we are always busy making slime. We were trying to make a little spending money and put some aside for college, so we decided to start selling slime. If you're interested in doing this too, we can help. There are many steps involved in creating a concept: purchasing supplies, making it, taking photos, listing it, packaging and posting it, etc. We quickly learned how this "little business" can turn into a full-time job.

Good packaging is essential to selling slime. Slime must be kept in an airtight container to prevent it from hardening. One of the most common forms of packaging is to use a 6- or 8-ounce plastic food container. One-ounce containers are often used for smaller orders. Some sellers prefer more durable plastic containers with screw-top lids, which may look more professional and provide more protection when shipping, but they also cost more and make your shipping package bulkier.

Our online shop is open 24/7, but school and homework come first, then activities and responsibilities at home. After those are complete, we fill orders and make stock. Weekends are our main restock days, when we make big batches of slime and prepackage them. We then list what we have available for

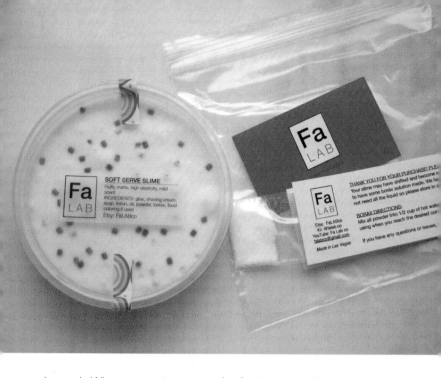

SOFT SERVE SLIME
Fluffy, matte, high elasticity, mild scent
INGREDIENTS: glue, shaving cream, soap, lotion, oil, powder, borax, food coloring if used
Etsy: FaLABco

THANK YOU FOR YOUR PURCHASE! PLE...
Your slime may have shifted and become ...
to have some borax solution made. We ha...
not need all the liquid so please store in ...

BORAX DIRECTIONS:
Mix all powder into 1/2 cup of hot wate...
using when you reach the desired con...

Etsy: FaLABco
IG: @falab.co
YouTube: Fa Lab co
falabco@gmail.com

Made in Las Vegas

If you have any questions or issues, ...

the week. When we receive orders, we check each product to refresh it, if needed, and then ship it out. We do list products that need to be made fresh upon ordering and, with those, we give ourselves up to three days to ship. Some slimes tend to become sticky during restocking or shipment, especially in warmer weather, so we try to make those fresh and provide borax powder in every order.

Proper shipping and handling is very important. Once an order is received, it goes through a process:

1. It is packed in our container, labeled, and then sealed with washi tape.
2. The container goes into a zip-top bag for extra freshness

and protection, along with a business card, an information sheet, and a half teaspoon of borax powder in a small baggie. The sheet gives instructions on using borax and when to use it.

3. The zip-top bag is then wrapped in paper with our logo sticker.

4. Then, the package is inserted into bubble mailers or a priority shipping box.

5. The shipping label is printed at home, directly via Etsy. The buyer chooses whether they want to use First Class, Priority, or Express shipping.

ENTREPRENEUR 101

In creating a name for our company, we wanted to make it original, professional, simple, and appealing to all ages. We named our company FaLAB. "Fa" stands for Fallon and Aspen. The "LAB" is our craft room, where we experiment and create new products. Our logo resembles an element from the periodic table. We did not want to restrict ourselves to selling slime so we left the word slime out of the name. We hope to be around after the slime trend ends and sell new creations. For now, however, we are busy enough with slime production.

Entering an already saturated market was daunting; we needed to be unique and think about the long term, as opposed to being a trendy shop. No matter what we sell, it is important for us to try and establish a brand. We had to be knowledgeable and have good customer service. Many people do not understand slime or know how to play with it, so educating new "slimers" is key to creating happy customers. Customer satisfaction is very important to us. These practices, along with being prepared to explain our products, their benefits, and how to use/play with slime provides a good foundation for any company.

When it comes to selling and marketing, Etsy is a great website for first-time sellers. It is easy to set up a shop, has its own search engine to bring traffic to your shop, tracks your sales and revenue, and provides statistics. Having a YouTube channel, Instagram account, or Facebook are great marketing tools and help direct customers to Etsy. Hosting pop-up shops in our community has increased our local sales and helped establish our good reputation among our

customers. These pop-ups also give us an opportunity to teach people about different slimes, how to play with them, and provides us with feedback.

PHOTOGRAPHING SLIME

These days, slime is not just goo in a cup. It needs to have good texture, proper elasticity, and look nice. Quality slime. It sounds like an oxymoron, but slime can be pretty too.

The photography bar is set very high on Etsy. You almost have to be a trained photographer to make your shop look professional. We don't have a photo studio or professional lighting, but we have learned that using natural light produces beautiful imagery. We always take our photos on a marble slab near the window in the mornings—do not use a flash since it will wash out colors and cause unnecessary shadows, as you can see below. The slime on the left was shot with a flash while the one on the right uses natural light.

Instagram is very visual as well; it is beneficial to have a good eye for design and to be able to style and compose artful photographs to attract buyers. Unique styling and composition is a standard that we set for

flash

natural light

our shop. Props and themes make our photographs more interesting. We try to focus on one slime at a time, but including several slimes in one photo makes a nice visual impact, as well. We love this creative part of the process as it allows us to see our simple slime in its final iteration.

Slime has became a huge Instagram hit over the past two years. People love to see other creations and watch slime videos from all over the world. An Instagram presence is a must for selling slime. Slime videos have evolved in the slime world, and we try our best to maintain this high visual standard in our videos and with the products we sell. It is best to record videos without background noise and to edit your videos before uploading.

CLEANUP

All good and slimy things must come to an end, but saying goodbye to your slime will be a whole lot easier with these cleanup tips.

- Clear your workspace before you begin measuring ingredients
- For slime parties, spread out a disposable plastic tablecloth to make cleanup easy
- It becomes easier to wash glue off your tools after soaking them in warm water
- Prepare a big bowl of water to soak your measuring cups after you use them to avoid a big sticky mess
- If your slime gets stuck to your clothes or carpet—or even your hair—remove as much slime as possible, soak with distilled vinegar, and then rinse with clean water
- Keep your old slime and use it to pick up sticky slime remnants, microbeads, and spilled glitter from your workspace
- You can even use slime to clean dust off your computer keyboard!
- If you store your slime in airtight bags, instead of reusable containers, it will be much easier to throw away your old slime

WHERE TO BUY SUPPLIES

- Discount stores
- Dollar stores
- Hardware stores
- Craft stores
- Toy stores

- Home improvement stores
- Drug stores
- Fabric stores
- Office supply stores
- Novelty stores

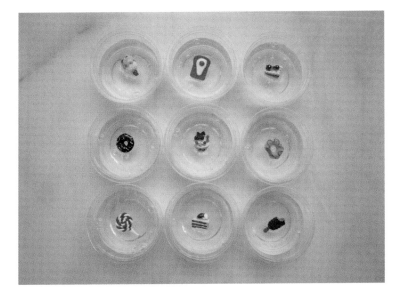

GLOSSARY

Activator—A thickening agent containing the borate ion (this can come from powdered borax dissolved in water; boric acid, found in liquid starch and certain brands of laundry detergent; or sodium tetraborate, found in contact lens solution) that turns liquid into semi-solid slime.

Autonomous Sensory Meridian Response (ASMR)—A feeling of blissful relaxation or meditative state triggered by sounds like whispering, quiet tapping, and the pops and crunches slime makes when you (or someone on YouTube) play with it. Not everyone experiences it; consider yourself lucky if you do.

Baking Soda—A household chemical (bicarbonate of soda) that has many uses. It reacts with the acidic solution (activator) in slime to make it more solid. Most recipes with contact solution will also call for baking soda.

Base—A substance containing polyvinyl acetate (PVA), most commonly glue, that is used to make slime.

Borax—Used in powder form for laundry and household cleaning, this chemical is found in many detergents, some brands of contact solution, and liquid starch. It reacts with the chemical PVA.

Butter Slime—Soft, dry, spreadable slime with minimal ASMR.

Contact Lens Solution—Saline solution that lists either boric acid or sodium borate in the ingredients can be used as an activator in slime.

Clear Slime—Transparent slime with loud clicks.

Clear-Based Floam—Transparent slime with Styrofoam beads that make loud, crunchy noises.

Fishbowl Slime—Usually a clear-based slime that has clear, circular, plastic beads that give the slime crunchy noises.

Fluffy Slime—An opaque slime that is stretchy, airy, and soft.

Glossy Slime—Also known as Milky Slime, this slime is stretchy, clicky, and glossy.

PVA Glue—Glue containing polyvinyl acetate, a chemical that reacts with borax, and makes slime. Glues with PVC include craft glue, carpenter's glue, all-purpose glue (such as Elmer's), wood glue, and others.

Shaving Cream—Used to make fluffy slime. The "foamy" style works best. It absobs moisture, and as a result the slime is a little firmer and a lot fluffier.

Soft Serve Slime—A matte, fluffy, and stretchy slime with good thwocks.

White-Based Floam—Fluffy slime with Styrofoam beads that make minimal crunchy sounds.

NOTES

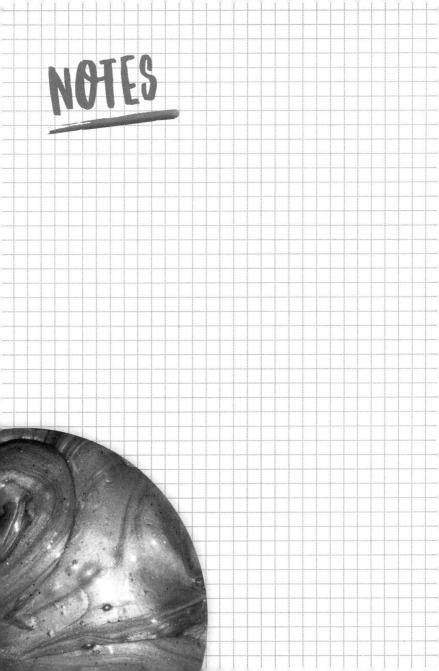

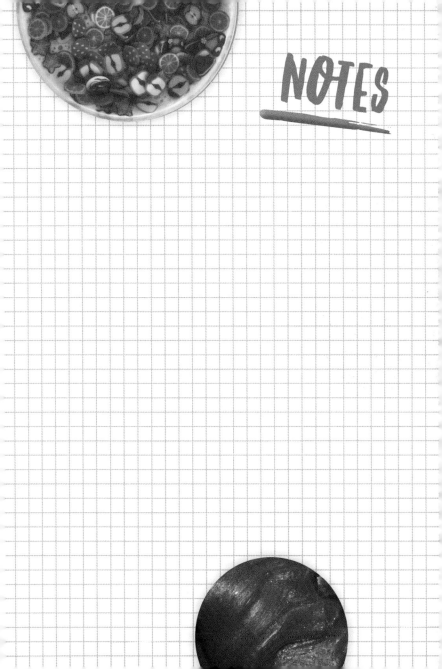

NOTES

NOTES

NOTES